Original title:
Through Tropical Waters

Copyright © 2025 Creative Arts Management OÜ
All rights reserved.

Author: Maya Livingston
ISBN HARDBACK: 978-1-80581-594-5
ISBN PAPERBACK: 978-1-80581-121-3
ISBN EBOOK: 978-1-80581-594-5

The Siren's Soothing Call

A fish flaunts its scales, all slippery and bright,
It wiggles and dances, what a silly sight!
The mermaids nearby just giggle and swish,
While trying to catch their favorite fish!

Secrets of the Azure Abyss

Down where the squid and octopus play,
They throw ink parties at the end of the day.
But watch out for clowns, with balloons in a trap,
The fish laugh so hard, they can hardly find a nap!

Driftwood and Distant Shores

The logs float by with tales of their own,
Whispering secrets, like a talking phone.
Crabs waste no time to have sandcastle fights,
While seagulls above are planning their flights!

Sheltered by the Palm Shade

Under the palms, a world very strange,
Where coconuts giggle, oh, how they change!
They drop from the trees, roll far and wide,
While beachgoers dodge them, eyes open, they hide!

Sky and Sea Collide

The seagulls squawk with flair,
While the fish swim with a dare.
Under clouds in bright parade,
Sunshine's laughter won't degrade.

With flip-flops lost to a wave,
My sunscreen's a sticky grave.
Sandy snacks are all the rage,
Seashells whisper, 'Turn the page.'

Glistening Shores of Velvet Sand

My flip-flops still perched on high,
As jellyfish drift on by.
Kids giggle with sticky hands,
While crabs dance in tiny bands.

A picnic turns to messy fight,
Burgers playing hide and fright.
Seagulls eye my fries with glee,
Snack time's quite a sight to see.

The Heartbeat of the Reef

Coral castles, bright and bold,
Invite fish to spin and scold.
Bubbles burst in silly cheer,
An octopus waves 'Hello, dear!'.

Underwater disco ball,
Turtles grooving, having a ball.
A clownfish strolls with flair and style,
Dancing away with a cheeky smile.

Waves of Forgotten Lullabies

The ocean sings a salty song,
As folks bob along, far too long.
Surfboards tumble, what a sight!
While dolphins giggle in pure delight.

Every splash, a playful tease,
Hidden treasures, if you please.
Sharks in shades swim by with grace,
While mermaids laugh and join the race.

The Rhythm of an Endless Horizon

Bobbing boats with silly hats,
Riding waves like acrobats.
Seagulls squawk and dive for fries,
As fish swim by in strange disguise.

Splashing laughter fills the air,
Life's a beach, without a care.
Sandy toes and sunburned dreams,
Floating on our sun-kissed beams.

Reflections in a Crystal Pool

Ducks in shades look quite absurd,
Flipping coins to see the bird.
Fins are flapping, quite a show,
What a world down below!

Mermaids giggle, tails all twirl,
Waves invite a splashy whirl.
Sun-kissed cheeks and salty hair,
We laugh and splutter, unaware.

Castaways of the Serene Deep

Shipwrecked dreams on floating beds,
Talking crabs give fashion spreads.
Coconuts stringed up in style,
Napping sharks with toothy smiles.

Island life is quite the prank,
Pirate jokes and treasure banks.
Plantains in silly hats are served,
While lost at sea, we're all preserved.

Flutter of Sea Turtles above Coral Gardens

Turtles glide in slow-mo race,
Bubbles make a silly face.
Coral reefs wear polka dots,
A clownfish laughs at tangled knots.

Napping on the ocean floor,
In a treasure chest, we snore.
Waves are like our giggly songs,
In this place where all belong.

Driftwood Dreams adrift

A piece of wood floats by me,
With stories deep as the sea.
I asked it why it's all alone,
It said, 'I'm just lost; I've become a drone!'

A seagull perched on my newfound friend,
Said, 'Life's a drift, no reason to bend!
We float on waves and soak in the sun,
Join the party, oh isn't it fun?'

The Dance of Silken Fins

The fish are dressed up in bright array,
Swirling and twirling, come join the fray!
One bumps a coral and shouts with glee,
'Hey, watch it, buddy, you're stepping on me!'

They spin around with a flick and a wink,
Saying, 'We're just here to swim and to drink!'
With bubbles released, a giggle erupts,
In their underwater ball, who's ever disrupted?

Beneath the Island's Embrace

On sandy shores, the crabs had a race,
With shells as their helmets, it's all such a chase!
One shouted, 'Outta my way, I'm a jet!'
But tripped on a flip-flop, you won't forget!

The pelicans cheered, a judge standing high,
With beaks like a gavel, they're tough, oh my!
They declared a winner, oh what a scene,
Too bad it was just a rogue tangerine!

Murmurs of the Ocean's Heart

The waves sing songs of mischief and cheer,
Whispering tales only fish can hear.
One wave said, 'Hey, let's prank that big boat,'
'Splash cannonball style, let's gloat and float!'

A dolphin swung by, laughing with flair,
'You call that a splash? You're hardly a scare!'
With a flick of a tail, they made quite a mark,
Splashing the sailors until it got dark!

Mirage of a Dreaming Coast

On sandy shores, the crabs do dance,
Wearing tiny shades, they take a chance.
A seagull laughs, drops a fishy treat,
And kids run faster, oh what a feat!

Sunburned tourists looking for shade,
Trying to find their lost flip-flop brigade.
Lemonade spills, the ice cream melts,
While jellyfish float, like spirits felt.

A dolphin pokes just to say hi,
And scares a swimmer who's feeling spry.
The beach ball bounces, heads collide,
In this grand circus, we all abide.

The sunset glows like a giant peach,
As sandcastles tumble, what a breach!
With laughter ringing and waves that froth,
We'll chase the tide, oh, what a broth!

Journey's End in the Embrace of Waves

At dock, we stumble, our ship's in sight,
The captain's hat seems a bit too tight.
Blowing kisses to the ocean breeze,
While fish play tag, just doing as they please.

We sail away, the seagulls squawk,
As crew serenades with a silly talk.
The compass spins, oh what a fright,
Was it north or south? What feels just right?

A mermaid grins, what a sight to see,
Waving her tail, she giggles with glee.
We toss her snacks, she flips in delight,
Our journey's end is within our sight.

Swells of laughter ride on the surf,
As dolphins jump, they show off their turf.
With every splash and each silly cheer,
Our wild ride ends, we've nothing to fear!

Song of the Ocean's Heart

The ocean hums a goofy tune,
With starfish dancing under the moon.
A fish named Fred wears polka dots,
Making a splash in tangled knots.

Turtles glide by, so slow and grand,
While crabs all march, a little band.
They sing of seaweed, sun, and fun,
A party under the golden sun.

A clam sings low, a whale sings high,
As pirates stumble and fish go by.
The rhythm flows, a bubble parade,
In this watery world, our worries fade.

With each wave crash, the giggles grow,
As sailors trip in the bubbly flow.
Our hearts are light, full of glee,
In the ocean's song, we're wild and free!

Life Amongst the Anemones

Dancing like a fish does,
In a bright coral bus.
Tickling tentacles sway,
Who knew sea life could play?

Clownfish with a silly grin,
Dodge every wave and spin.
Squid's doing a strange jig,
Man, that shrimp's got a big gig!

Starfish lounging all day,
Sunbathing in their own way.
Anemones throw a bash,
Now there's a jellyfish splash!

Who knew the sea's a hoot,
Where crabs wear dancing boots?
What joy in every wave,
In this anemone rave!

Murmurs of the Mangroves

In the twist of tangled trees,
A parrot sneezes with ease.
Loud frogs proclaim it's a party,
While the iguana feels hearty.

Crabs in suits look so dapper,
Dance to the rhythm, oh how they caper.
Mosquitoes buzzing a tune,
Guess they heard it's a boon!

A fish swings by on a vine,
Chilling out, sipping brine.
Guess this low tide's the place,
For an undersea embrace!

Murmurs echo, spirits soar,
In this mangrove dance floor.
Who's inviting the sun to play?
A perfect end to a silly day!

The Call of Distant Horizons

Waves whisper secrets to the shore,
Shells giggle as they ask for more.
Seagulls in wacky capes,
Look like they're daring shapes!

Sunsets painting skies in gold,
Every glance feels bold.
Mermaids join the revelry,
Chanting sweetly, 'Come dance with me!'

A friendly dolphin makes a splash,
Trying to join in the bash.
But who knew he'd slip and roll?
Now he's the sea's own stroll!

Horizons call with silly glee,
Promising a world so free.
Let's make a splash, dance and dive,
In this funny ocean jive!

Underwing of a Pelican

Under a pelican's wide wing,
We marvel at the fun it brings.
Fish flip, diving in disbelief,
As the bird sips on ocean leaf!

With a belly like a sack,
He swoops in and makes a snappy crack.
Plop! Fish go boink and giggle,
While the sea stars start to wiggle.

A crab shimmies, putting on a show,
While seahorses dance in a row.
What's that? A shoe on the scene?
Oh no! It's just a seaweed dream!

Under the waving gusts, we cheer,
At the antics that draw us near.
With laughter echoing like a song,
Here where the ocean creatures belong!

Secrets of the Reef

The fish all wear their brightest hue,
They gossip as they swim on through.
Coral castles, grand and bright,
Hold secrets that escape the light.

A crab in shades of pink and gold,
Tells tales of treasure that he sold.
With bubbles popping, laughter's found,
As quirky creatures dance around.

A parrotfish with silly grace,
Wears a goofy smile on his face.
He chews on coral like it's gum,
A silly sight, oh what a fun!

The sea anemone waves a hand,
Inviting all to join the band.
With jellyfish doing the twist,
Who would've thought they'd be on a list?

Journey to the Hidden Isles

We set sail with a clatter and cheer,
On a boat that smelled of last night's beer.
The map is drawn in crayon bright,
But pirates don't seek treasures at night!

A dolphin jumps, it kicks up a splash,
While seagulls caw and make a dash.
We spot an island shaped like a shoe,
Maybe they have snacks or a barbecue!

Mermaids sing out from the shore,
With voices making our ears sore.
But they offer coconuts and fun,
We laugh and dance under the sun.

Suddenly, a crab joins our crew,
He's the captain, who knew it was true?
He claims the treasure's some salty fries,
We let out giggles, oh how time flies!

Tidepool Tranquility

In a tide pool, life is a game,
Tiny creatures without any shame.
A starfish casually strikes a pose,
While a snail crawls slowly, sniffing a rose.

A hermit crab scuttles with charm,
Trading shells, he means no harm.
Here, laughter bubbles like foamy seas,
As sea cucumbers wiggle with ease.

The seaweed dances to an unheard beat,
While clams play hide and seek at our feet.
Fish sing tales of adventures grand,
All while stuck in their sandy land.

The tide whispers jokes of the deep blue,
With shellfish giggling in a merry stew.
We chuckle and splash, oh what a sight,
In our tidepool of delights, pure light!

Celestial Navigation

The stars above twinkle like eyes,
Guiding us on with their playful lies.
A night sky, a sailor's dream,
We laugh as we plot our silly scheme.

Constellations dance in the dark,
A moonlit path, a swaying lark.
We point to Orion, then to a crab,
Navigating with laughter, it's not a drab.

A fish-shaped cloud floats overhead,
It whispers secrets we've never read.
We sail through giggles, through dreams untold,
As the sea sprawls out, vast and bold.

With every wave springs a chorus of glee,
In this ocean of fun, we learn to be free.
Stars overhead, and we're full of cheer,
With every splash, we conquer our fear!

Pastel Dusk on a Quiet Bay

The sun dips low, a peachy fright,
Crabs dance under the fading light.
A fish in shades both bright and bold,
Says, "Catch me if you can, I'm sold!"

The seagulls squawk their evening tune,
While dolphins frolic, making a boon.
One fish, wearing a tiny hat,
Claims he's the king; oh, imagine that!

With jokes about the size of tides,
The octopus shows off his slides.
A beach ball bounces, laughter flows,
As flip-flops trip and confidence goes!

Beneath the sky, in colors rare,
Life's silly moments fill the air.
A sunset dip in silly cheer,
As night draws near, we hold our beer!

The Glistening Path of Shells

Upon the sand, the shells do gleam,
A snail in disco, what a dream!
Hopping crabs think they can outrun,
But slippery shoes spoil all the fun!

A clam shouts, "I'm a rockstar, see!"
The starfish says, "Come dance with me!"
But twirling while you lack a spine,
Can lead to woes, like not a line!

Some fish parade in ridiculous hats,
While searching for those elusive spats.
"Why wear a shell?" a jelly asked,
"I'm cool enough with my wobbly mask!"

As the tide rolls in, we trip and slide,
In this glistening place where laughter hides.
With shells galore and a song to tell,
All join the dance on this coastal shell!

Dreams Carried by Coastal Breezes

The wind whispers tales of happy days,
While seaweed wiggles in funny ways.
A boat named 'Floater' drifts in glee,
Riding the breeze, it's wild and free!

Seagulls plotting their snack attack,
Bargain with fish for a tasty pack.
A pelican snickers, 'You're too slow!'
With fishy breath, he steals the show!

In the shade, a sunbather snores,
While waves tickle the sandy shores.
"Hey, watch my drink!" a kid does shout,
As a sneaky crab pulls it out!

Dreams float in with the salty air,
As laughter and chaos blend with flair.
Here under the sun, all worries cease,
Just silly moments, the sweetest peace!

Beneath the Glimmering Surface

Bubbles rise like giggles in the sea,
Where fish wear wigs saying, "Look at me!"
A sea cucumber joins in the chase,
Swaying and dancing, it finds its place!

Octopuses juggling shells top-notch,
While starfish clap, trying not to botch.
A clownfish swims with an inflatable,
Shrieking, "Life's just a big festival!"

Beneath the waves, a dance-off starts,
With crabs showing off their twisty arts.
They shuffle and jive, oh what a sight,
As sea turtles groan, "We'll dance tonight!"

With bubbles bursting in happy sounds,
The ocean floor becomes fun-filled grounds.
As laughter bubbles, life's joy unfolds,
In this whimsical world where silliness holds!

Fluid Journeys of the Soul

Bubbles float like silly ghosts,
As fish perform their ocean boast.
Waves are laughing, tides are playing,
The seaweed dance is quite displaying.

Jellyfish juggle, what a sight!
Crabs doing the cha-cha in the moonlight.
Seashells gossip with a pinch of salt,
'What's this tide doing? It's a jolt!'

Penguins in flip-flops on sun-kissed rocks,
Playing tag with floating socks.
Mermaids twirling, they can't resist,
In this underwater, handstand twist!

The squid's got talent; it paints so bright,
With colors that twinkle, oh what a night!
Ocean giggles, bubbles burst,
These fluid journeys, oh what a thirst!

Coral Castles Beneath the Surface

In coral castles, conch shells rule,
Where starfish play the fool in pool.
Anemones wave like they're on a throne,
While clownfish tell jokes, never alone.

A sea cucumber hosts a quirky feast,
With sea lettuce rolls that a snail released.
The octopus is chef, a master of fun,
Whipping up tacos under the sun.

Turtles do yoga, all very zen,
Stretching their limbs like they're pro again.
Seahorses strut in a fashion parade,
While eels play the harp, all serenely displayed.

Undersea neighbors throw a big bash,
With jelly beans flying, oh what a splash!
Coral castles cheer with bubbly delight,
As fish toast to friendship, shimmering bright!

Colors of a Forgotten Lagoon

In a lagoon where colors sing,
Dolphins squeak and mermaids swing.
Old pirate ghosts tell tales of yore,
While crabs argue on the sandy floor.

Here, the clams have disco balls,
And sea turtles dance in fanciful halls.
Fish in wigs do the latest craze,
Making waves in the stylish bays.

A lazy seal suns with a grin,
While squids juggle, oh what a spin!
Bubblegum skies, candy cane shores,
Invite sea critters to open doors.

Life's a splash in vibrant hues,
With every ripple, a bit of muse.
In a forgotten lagoon, laughter's the key,
To treasure hunts of pure glee!

Symphony of the Salted Air

The salty breeze is a lively tune,
As crabs and seagulls dance under the moon.
Clams form a band, all dressed up nice,
Singing melodies that are quite precise.

The ocean plays drums with each wave's crash,
While fish conduct with a graceful splash.
A conch shell spills secrets, a whispering sound,
In the harmony of the salty ground.

Guitar sea cucumbers strum with ease,
As flounders twist to catch the breeze.
Every fin and flipper joins the choir,
Creating laughter that lifts us higher.

Dolphins leap into the high notes,
With a splash of joy that happily floats.
In this symphony, life's never dull,
As fish, fowl, and fun weave the incredible!

Twilight's Kiss on the Water's Edge

A crab in a tux, quite a sight,
Dances with a fish, oh what a fright!
They twirl on the sand, in moonlight's glow,
While seagulls swoop down for the show.

A dolphin plays tag with a floating shoe,
"Catch me if you can!" It sings out, too.
The seaweed waves like a crowd in cheer,
As shells giggle softly, oh dear, oh dear!

A starfish calls out, "I'm so glamorous!"
But really it's just a tad humorous.
With a wink and a nudge, it waves hello,
To a turtle who's munching on some sea foam.

So laugh with the tides, let your worries go,
Join the underwater ballet, put on a show!
With every splash, hear the ocean's song,
Life's a party, come dance along!

Sirens of Sunlit Shores

A mermaid with snacks lures sailors in,
"Join me for chips, let the fun begin!"
Her friends laugh and splash, they're quite a crew,
Eating fishy nachos, with a seaweed brew.

One sings a tune that's catchy and bright,
While crabs tap their claws in a comical fight.
The tide rolls in, bringing sea cucumber pies,
A feast for the senses, oh what a surprise!

With a wink and a giggle, the waves make their call,
"Gather 'round, folks! Join us, one and all!"
Drifting on floats made from driftwood and shells,
Together they tumble, oh how laughter swells!

As sunset paints skies with vibrant delight,
The sirens break out in a dance, oh what a sight!
With water balloons and a splash of coconut cream,
The shore holds a party, a whimsical dream!

Whispers of the Coral Deep

In the depths where the silly fish swim,
A clownfish declares, "Life's a whim!"
It dances with shrimp, makes silly faces,
While turtles roll 'round in hilarious races.

The octopus juggles, a sight to behold,
With shells and some seaweed, stories retold.
"It's all in the grip!" he laughs with glee,
Dodging the angler with the sparkly key.

A pufferfish pouts, "I'm too square for this!"
While others just giggle at what they miss.
A sea sponge giggles, "You'll fit in just fine!"
As they twirl and they shout, "Let's have a good time!"

So dive into laughter where corals reside,
With whispers and chuckles, let joy be your guide.
In this underwater realm, life's never too steep,
With friendships so silly, the ocean's a leap!

Luminous Currents

A jellyfish glows like a disco ball,
Floating like royalty, it welcomes all.
"Join the dance, don't be shy!" it breezes,
While sea cucumbers wobble, like jelly cheeses.

A school of fish performs the conga line,
With bubbles and giggles, oh how they shine!
The eel plays the drums with a rockstar flair,
While crabs pull the strings, do they care? Oh rare!

With a flip and a twist, the wave dancers sway,
Caught in the rhythm, they're here to play.
From the depths of the sea to the sun-lit heights,
Life's a grand circus, filled with delights!

So splash down the currents, ride waves filled with cheer,
In this ocean adventure, there's nothing to fear.
With laughter as bright as the stars up above,
Join in the fun, it's a celebration of love!

Basking in Celestial Waters

In a sea of sunscreen and laughter,
We float like fish in silly hats.
The crabs dance with a diva's flair,
While seagulls steal our beachside snacks.

Waves tickle our toes as we splash,
A coconut floats, a pirate's prize.
With a splash! A seal takes a dive,
Catching our breath with surprise!

Sandcastles rise, then collapse fast,
As we munch on chips with glee.
A jellyfish joins our sun-soaked game,
Doing the worm—who knew it swam free?

Finally, the sun sets below,
We marvel at the colors' burst.
What a day for fun in the warm glow,
Mirthful moments in tropical firsts!

Cradle of the Blue Horizon

The ocean's a playground for the brave,
We ride the waves with squeals of delight.
A dolphin pranks us, oh what a wave!
Surely it thinks it's quite the sight!

Wobbly surfboards, we roll and we flop,
Each tumble brings laughter to the sky.
A sea turtle joins and says, "Don't stop!"
"Surf's up, dudes!" it seems to imply!

Beach balls fly in a colorful arc,
While sunscreen battles with a cold drink.
We chase the tide from dawn until dark,
And wonder what fish must think!

As we gather seashells, oh what a score,
A clam and a starfish start to prance.
We join the dance, who could want more?
Living so silly in a summer trance!

Embrace of the Distant Isle

On a boat made of dreams, we sail away,
As parrots steal our tropical hats.
Mango juice spills, oh, what a display,
When iguanas join and chit-chat!

Palm trees wave in a rhythm divine,
Each misstep brings giggles of glee.
A crab in sunglasses sips on brine,
"Living the life, just look at me!"

Up in the trees, a monkey swings,
Tossing coconuts as a friendly tease.
We laugh as the coconut-king sings,
With such antics, who wouldn't be pleased?

As the sun dips low, our hearts feel light,
We toast with shells—what a silly sight!
In this whimsical world of soft, bright dreams,
Life's a joke, bursting with sunbeam schemes!

The Rhythm of Pelagic Life

With our fins and flippers, we dive in style,
Disco fish dance in the coral scene.
Worms do the twist; it's all quite worthwhile,
An underwater party is truly serene!

A clownfish swims with a joke to share,
"Why don't lobsters ever get lost?"
They point to the seaweed without a care,
"Because they always follow the 'tossed'!"

Starfish lounge as if on vacation,
While the seaweed sways to our silly tunes.
We sway together in joyful elation,
Under the gaze of the laughing moons.

As bubbles rise and our spirits soar,
We giggle and splash till the tide calls us home.
What a delight, this ocean galore,
In the sea's rhythm, we happily roam!

Fleeting Hues at Dusk

The sun dips low, a splash of gold,
Fish make faces, daring and bold.
Crabs dance sideways, oh what a sight,
As seaweed twirls in the fading light.

A parrotfish giggles, wearing a grin,
While starfish plot a new way to spin.
The tide rolls in with a cheeky push,
As shells whisper secrets, gone in a hush.

Clowns in the coral paint so bright,
Jellyfish jiggle, quite a delight.
As dolphins chuckle, doing their tricks,
The whole ocean laughs with comedic flicks.

So let's raise a fin to this watery fun,
Where colors blend under the setting sun.
With bubbles of laughter floating around,
In the grand underwater playground found.

Beneath the Wave's Embrace

Beneath the waves, where oddballs play,
An octopus winks, then swims away.
Sea cucumbers lounge with lazy flair,
While sea turtles take selfies, unaware.

Crabs wear top hats, what a fine show,
As clams gossip soft and flow.
A fish in a suit, quite underdressed,
With pearls of wisdom, he's feeling blessed.

Anemones dance with each gentle sway,
While seahorses gossip and giggle away.
The murky depths hide treasures galore,
And seaweed tickles, who could want more?

So dive on down, let the foolishness start,
Where every creature has a funny part.
In the splashy embrace of the ocean's delight,
There's whimsy and joy, all through the night.

Wanderlust in Aquatic Realms

In the depths of blue, explorers roam,
Pufferfish puff with a cheeky foam.
They wear funny hats and capricious frowns,
As they frolic through aquatic towns.

A vibrant clownfish trip traps and flips,
While lazy seals plan their holiday trips.
The coral dances, a colorful show,
As sea urchins giggle from below.

Swimming with glee, a dolphin team,
Plays tag with mermaids in a shared dream.
In this charm-filled world where laughter floats,
Every wave carries quirky little notes.

So pack your fins and swim along,
In the ocean's orchestra, join the song.
With underwater laughter that echoes so sweet,
Wanderlust surfaces, in every heartbeat.

The Color of Venturing Souls

With a flip and a swirl, the ocean's alive,
Squid throw confetti, making a dive.
The seahorses prance in their breezy ballet,
While crabs march forward in silly array.

Bright parrotfish gossip over a shell,
Echoing secrets from the ocean floor well.
As they splash and they giggle, driftwood their stage,
Life under the sea is a vibrant page.

Turtles take turns on a reef-side slide,
Taking the plunge with laughable pride.
In this wacky world where colors swirl bright,
Every venture is a comical flight.

So join the parade in this oceanic feast,
Where smiles abound, from the greatest to least.
With each wave that crashes, let laughter unfold,
In the colorful tales of the sea to be told.

The Gentle Lure of the Lagoon

In the lagoon, the fish swim by,
Throwing shade, saying 'Oh my!'
With nets and laughter, we make our play,
Snagging a crab who simply won't stay.

The sun hangs low, we're feeling bold,
A floating burger, if truth be told.
But watch out for the splashing seals,
They steal our snacks with cheeky squeals!

A pelican dives, oh what a sight,
Missed the fish, and that's all right.
We'll just keep laughing, get wet and wild,
The lagoon's a playground, sweet and mild.

With floaties and friends, cheers fill the air,
An epic day, without a care.
So raise your drinks, and let's explore,
The gentle lure, we cannot ignore!

Dancing in the Wake of Dolphins

Dolphins leap with joyful flair,
While I try hard not to spill my pear!
They whirl and twirl, such graceful glee,
I splash and crash, 'Please swim with me!'

Their smiles are wide, teeth gleaming bright,
I mimic moves, but what a sight!
I slip and slide, and then I splash,
A dolphin giggles, a fishy bash!

They point and tease with playful tricks,
I'm flailing about, needing a fix.
But oh, the fun, despite my plight,
In the wake of dolphins, life feels right!

So let's dance, with fins and feet,
In a watery world, it's quite the treat.
With laughter echoing off each wave,
Dancing together, we find our brave!

Portrait of a Sunset Beach

The sun dips low, a vibrant hue,
As I try to paint with a splattered shoe!
My canvas shifts, the tide rolls in,
With every wave, my art's a spin.

Seagulls dance in the sky so bold,
My sandwich snatched, oh, how it's sold!
The colors mix with salty air,
As I chase that bird without a care.

The beach ball bounces, it flies away,
I chase it down, oh what a play!
Tripping over sandcastles high,
Creating chaos under the sky.

With laughter shared, the evening glows,
A sunset portrait, cheeky woes.
We leave with memories and grains of sand,
On this silly beach, nothing's bland!

Drifting Along the Gentle Flow

A raft floats softly, just take a seat,
With snacks galore, it can't be beat!
But watch for the splash from a giggling friend,
As we drift along, it's fun without end.

The current pulls us, oh what a ride,
With rubber ducks, we're filled with pride.
A fish jumps up; I shout and squeak,
Is that a dolphin or just a peak?

We sing silly songs to the rhythm of waves,
When someone trips, and splashes like knaves.
With drinks in hand, we float and glide,
As laughter echoes, we savor the tide.

So join this journey, come float with me,
In waters so warm, wild and free.
With chuckles and splashes, we lose track of time,
Drifting along, life feels so sublime!

Nurtured by Celestial Currents

In the pool of the ocean blue,
Fish wear sunglasses, what a view!
Sea turtles race like they're on a spree,
While crabs do the cha-cha with glee.

Dolphins dive, taking a leap,
Mermaids giggle, secrets to keep.
Seashells gossip on the bright shore,
They give all the updates—who could ask for more?

Jellyfish dance, a wobbly show,
With lasers lighting up their glow.
Underwater, it's a carnival spree,
Where even the octopus wants to be free!

So join the wave, let laughter swell,
In this silly sea, you'll know me well.
Adventure awaits in each splashy prance,
Grab your snorkel, it's time to dance!

The Breath of Fen and Foam

In the marsh where the frogs sing,
Where turtles skate like it's a fling!
A pelican dons a party hat,
While an otter ponders where it's at.

Mosquitoes line up for a ball,
In the swamp, there's joy for all.
With bubbles popping, laughter's loud,
As the reeds sway and join the crowd.

The crickets chirp a nightly tune,
As the stars dance out, over the dune.
Frogs croak jokes; they're quite the team,
In this watery dream, laughter's the theme!

So wade on in, it's quite a scene,
You never know where you might glean.
A splash of fun, a giddy fright,
In the breath of fen, everything's right!

Capturing the Crescendo of Breaches

Whales with hats, a daring crew,
Leaping high, oh what a view!
They splash down, with a wink and grin,
As dolphins cheer, they join in the din.

A fish with flair starts a game,
While an octopus dresses the same.
They raise the stakes with style and fun,
Making waves till the day is done.

The sea's alive with a bustling beat,
Each breach a burst, it can't be beat.
With underwater selfies, fish strike poses,
Life's a show, as everyone knows it!

So grab your fins and join the ride,
In this watery world, laughter's our guide.
In the frothy rush, joy can't be seized,
As we celebrate life with fun and ease!

Footprints in Sandy Serenity

On the shore, where the sun does bake,
Footprints tell stories, for goodness' sake!
Seagulls squawk with a cheeky tone,
While crabs play hide-and-seek alone.

Sandcastles rise, mighty and grand,
With moats that could rival any land.
A jellyfish strolls, oh what a sight,
Waving to beachgoers, feeling quite bright!

Kids chase the waves, scream with delight,
As shells roll in, what a funny sight!
They gather treasures, only to find,
A rubber ducky left behind!

So frolic with joy, let laughter lead,
In sandy serenity, we're all freed.
Dance with the tides, embrace the fun,
For every footprint tells a tale, one by one!

Dance of the Sapphire Tides

Bubbles rise, fish in disguise,
Dance in circles, oh what a surprise!
A crab with claws like a duke,
Sips on seaweed, feeling quite kooky.

Jellyfish waltz in electric hues,
While turtles wear their best scuba shoes.
A dolphin juggles a coconut,
While sea urchins laugh, that silly nut!

Starfish twirl in a cosmic spin,
With seahorses laughing, they pull you in.
The rhythm of waves, a clumsy beat,
As octopuses tap dance on their feet.

Bubbles pop, the party's in full swing,
A crab in a tuxedo starts to sing.
With laughter echoing through the tide,
The ocean's a stage, where the silly reside!

Echoes Beneath the Sea

In the depths where the secrets hide,
A fish recounts tales with great pride.
His friends all giggle, fins all a-flap,
As he spins yarns in a gurgly clap.

"Once I saw a shark in a hat,
Trying to catch a well-dressed cat!"
The flush of a clownfish, laughter ignites,
As sea turtles ponder all the delights.

An eel slithers by with a wink,
In the light of a sunset, what do you think?
"Pirates? Nonsense!" a seahorse will say,
"Just lost seaweed on a very bad day!"

With bubbles bursting, tales come alive,
Echoes of laughter, oh how they thrive!
In the watery world, fun's the decree,
Where every wave brings a new jubilee.

Reflections on Aquatic Dreams

Reflecting upon the shimmering waves,
A fish dreams of honors and briny knaves.
"Who needs a crown when you're velvety bright?
I'm the king of the kelp, what a marvelous sight!

Beneath the Canopy of Waves

Beneath the canopy where bright colors play,
The fish throw shade in a stylish ballet.
They wear tiny goggles and swim with flair,
And sea cucumbers wave from their cozy lair.

Anemones dance to the rhythm of tide,
As crabs host a beach ball, a nautical ride.
"Oh dear, not another seaweed surprise!"
They giggle as fish dive to the deep blue skies.

Blowfish puff up, hoping to impress,
But they tumble and roll in a comical mess.
With laughter that ebbs like a wave's gentle breath,
Life's a splash of fun, even in depth!

Embracing the Ocean's Breath

The fish wear ties and dance a jig,
Octopus in shades, that's quite the fig.
Seagulls squawk with laughter loud,
While crabs perform for the beach crowd.

Waves tickle toes like a playful beast,
Sun-tanned turtles join the feast.
A conch shell calls, 'Join the fun!'
Mermaids splashing, on the run!

Fins and flippers all unite,
Underwater antics, a silly sight.
Sharks in bowties, striking a pose,
As dolphins do the limbo, goodness knows!

The seaweed giggles, a silly green,
In every bubble, a chuckle is seen.
So raise a shell and take a sip,
In these waters, let's do the flip!

Enchanted Shores of Serenity

A crab named Larry sings off-key,
While clams debate who's royalty.
Sandcastles rise, then tumble down,
The beach is buzzing like a circus town.

Seashells gossip, they're quite pretentious,
With starfish posing, oh so contentious.
The waves roll in with a playful wink,
"Do you need floaties?" they lovingly think.

Pelicans dive for fish in a line,
Missed each time - oh, isn't that fine?
While blowfish puff in a silly way,
Creating laughter at the end of the day.

Surfboards dance, doing the cha-cha,
With seals on logs, it's a grand gala.
Even the piña coladas giggle,
From a coconut, they loving wiggle!

The Soliloquy of the Sea

The salty breeze brings tales to tell,
Of a whale who slipped and fell.
Crabs roll over in fits of glee,
At the antics of jellyfish, full of spree.

A fish with glasses reads a book,
Pausing to check the way that they look.
Sea cucumbers throw a fashion show,
With starfish cheering, "Dude, you glow!"

Turtles in flip-flops, what a sight,
Grooving under the moonlight.
While clams debate the best dance move,
Claiming in water, they really groove.

Waves whisper jokes about the shore,
As dolphins chuckle, wanting more.
Ocean tides join in the fun,
At the dusk of day, under the sun!

Silent Reveries of the Seaweed

The seaweed sways like a hippy's hair,
In a dance-off, it has no care.
Sponges watch, with bulging eyes,
As they learn to feast on ocean fries.

A fish with an ukulele sings,
About underwater flings and bling.
Barnacles join in with their own beat,
Clapping shells to the joyful heat.

Anemones twirl, all colors bright,
While seahorses gossip deep in the night.
The coral joins with a shimmy and shake,
Inviting everyone for a fun ocean break.

Shrimps share secrets, oh what a sight,
While eels show off, even in fright.
In this sea of laughs and delight,
Every splash brings joy, oh, what a night!

Serpentines of Salt and Light

A fish once danced with a crab in tow,
They spun and twirled, putting on a show.
The octopus laughed, legs flailing wide,
While seahorses giggled and swayed with pride.

A clam then freestyled, just as he could,
But tripped on a shell, feeling misunderstood.
The waiter was a turtle, slow but spry,
He served up seaweed with a wink and a sigh.

Jellyfish joined with a glowing glow,
But got tangled up—what a comedic flow!
They floated around with a colorful plight,
In this watery realm of salt and light.

So if you swim where the laughter's rife,
Join in the dance, it's a slippery life.
Embrace the waves, let your joy ignite,
Where creatures perform in their own delight.

The Language of the Sea Breeze

The ocean whispered to a big ol' whale,
Who thought it was speaking in secret detail.
He cherished the gossip, oh what a treat,
As he shared it with fish at the coral street.

A crab, with his chatter, liked to critique,
He planned his remarks at the end of the week.
But each time he'd speak, he'd just click and clack,
Leaving all of the fish in a laughter-filled wrack.

The dolphin chimed in with a flip and a twist,
Yet he slipped on a wave and fell in a mist.
"Not the best timing!" yelled a seagull above,
As the sun set, they shared stories of love.

So if you listen to the breezy refrain,
You might find a giggle mixed in with the rain.
In the language of waves, where the whispers tease,
You'll find all the joy in the sea breeze.

Upon the Glistening Tide

Upon the shimmering waves, what a sight,
A school of fish swam, all darting in flight.
They played hide and seek amongst rocks and sand,
While crabs in the shallows plotted their stand.

"Let's have a race!" cried a starfish on deck,
But twisted his arms, what a slippery wreck!
The crowd, oh so amused, broke out in giggles,
As the starfish waved, doing funny wiggles.

A pelican swooped, looking quite grand,
But mistook a small fish for a morsel at hand.
He fumbled and tumbled, what a good laugh,
While fish all around chimed, "What a miscalculation, half!"

High tides bring treasures, like laughter and cheer,
So join in the fun, as the good times draw near.
In the dance of the sea, where silliness slides,
Life glows with joy upon glistening tides.

Rippled Memories of Sunsets

As the sun dipped low, colors danced and played,
A crab reminisced of the games he once laid.
"Remember the time I wore seaweed as hat?"
He burst into laughter, his friends joined in that!

A dolphin proposed a wacky reunion,
But kept forgetting, what a funny distraction!
"Let's meet by the rocks at the break of dawn,"
He said, then flipped over, "Oops! Where have I gone?"

The seagulls swooped down with a caw and a spin,
"Throw us some chips, and let the fun begin!"
They gathered around, a buffet at dusk,
Nibbling and joking, it's friendship we trust.

Every ripple carried a soft sunset glow,
With tales of the sea that everyone knows.
So cherish these moments under fading light,
For laughter and love give the night its delight.

Colors of the Ocean Floor

A fish in a tutu swirls with glee,
Blowing bubbles, feeling fancy and free.
Corals that giggle, all painted bright,
Underwater parties last all night!

Squid do the cha-cha, and clams do a dance,
While starfish wink, giving love a chance.
The sea cucumber grins, oh what a show,
Underwater antics, a colorful glow!

Crabs with their top hats, what a strange sight,
Do they hold parties? I think they just might!
And the octopus juggles, what an amusing feat,
In this rainbow realm, life's a delicious treat!

Banana fish slip, trying not to crash,
While dolphin DJs spin records with sass.
Join this aquatic hullabaloo, take the plunge,
In this jolly ocean floor, we dance and we lunge!

In the Shadow of Coconut Palms

Beneath the palms where coconuts sway,
A parrot sings tunes to start the day.
Sandy beach blankets hide burrowing crabs,
While a tourist complains, 'I just lost my labs!'

Flip-flops make music with each silly step,
As a sunburnt whale claims a beachside rep.
Lizards in sunglasses lounge on the scene,
While ants throw a party, all dressed up in green!

A hammock swings low, with a giggle or two,
As a cat tries to nap, she's still in the queue.
Umbrellas are bouncing, drinks spill with flair,
Oh, the laughter and fun, floating lighter than air!

In the shade of the palms, life's a carefree jest,
With palms as our guides, we enjoy every fest.
Each day a new tale told under the sun,
With coconuts laughing, our hearts filled with fun!

Mariner's Heartbeat

On the deck of the ship, what a whimsical sight,
The captain spins yarns till the stars twinkle bright.
A seagull steals sandwiches, quite the rogue,
While the first mate just plays with a rubbery toad!

Oceans like jelly, wobbling with cheer,
Frogs in the rigging, oh dear, oh dear!
The compass spins wildly, it's a dizzy dance,
While sharks serenade with a seaweed romance!

The mariner's heart beats in sync with the tide,
Cheesy jokes flying, laughter cannot hide.
Sailors in a frenzy, trying to catch,
The fish that glow pink—what a colorful batch!

Anchors away, laughter rings through the air,
As the vessel bobs wildly without any care.
Together they sail, a mismatched crew,
In a comedy of oceans, life feels brand new!

Currents of the Human Soul

In waves of laughter, we find our delight,
As jellybeans tumble in crazy moonlight.
Fish wear bow ties, such elegant flair,
As humans and beings dance in the air!

The tides tell our secrets, stirring our minds,
A dolphin's sweet whisper, a truth that it finds.
With bubbles of joy and dreams made of foam,
We ride on the ripples, never alone!

Sunshine tickles toes, igniting our glee,
Sandcastles crumble, but we all agree.
In the ocean of laughter, our souls intertwine,
Floating on currents, life's a whimsical rhyme!

The shores keep our stories like shells on display,
With giggles and chuckles guiding our way.
These currents remind us, with every smile,
The humor of life makes the journey worthwhile!

www.ingramcontent.com/pod-product-compliance
Lightning Source LLC
Chambersburg PA
CBHW072135070526
44585CB00016B/1695